What others say...

"Greg's poems have been an inspiration to me. I've had many changes in my life and his poems have given me purpose and direction. Greg has uplifted many while skillfully communicating some of life's bittersweet verities. He speaks from the heart and has a God given talent which he shares with many. Love you Mr. Wooley! Keep up the good work!" ~ *Louise Hawthorne*

"When reading the words that Greg Wooley has written there is something magical that happens. Peace and reassurance are two words that come to mind. Peace that everything is temporary and reassurance that in and through God we are equipped. Greg's work has had a major impact on me professionally and personally! Thanks Greg" ~ *Anna Reed*

"There have been many times that I have read a poem from Gregory and it just seems to be so heart felt yet I feel as if I could relate in so many ways. They help remind me that life can be full of ups and downs and that if I stay the course it will come out positive in the end. Thank You Greg Wooley for your words of hope & love." ~ *Donnie Seward*

"God bestowed his grace on Greg. This Grace came with a gift of writing. And Greg shares his gift with us through poetry. Through his own journey, Greg has been able to pen his God given insights into writings, writings that can help each of us on our own paths in this life." ~ *Sylvia Carrier*

"Greg's intuitions became my into-wishing. This is a sign of rare soul-impacting poetry."
~ *Elizabeth Perrotta*

"Every sentence of Greg's poems is a haiku, a complete poem independently meaningful."
~ *Enzo Torre*

"Greg Wooley offers elegant, inspired prose filled with life's wisdom that may be enjoyed and understood by all who read it. Be swept along for the journey." ~ *Leslie Bertrand*

"The poems in Gems from God have inspired me on many a morning when I have needed some spiritual nourishment to help get me through my day.

I have shared some of the poems through social media with my friends who have also been inspired. The poems in this book are aptly called gems!"
~ *Robin Torillo*

"Greg's written words are filled with hope. It's the kind of hope that uplifts and touches the core of our being. His poems have moved me deeply because I resonate with them. Greg pours his heart into his words and it shows. Step into his world and let his words embrace you with spirit and uplift you." ~ *Mark Gai, Podcast Host and Storyteller*

GEMS FROM G.O.D.

Greg Wooley
Greater Ways Publishing

ISBN: 978-1-7339478-9-3 (paperback)
ISBN: 978-1-7339478-7-9 (case laminate)
ISBN: 978-1-7339478-8-6 (kindle)

Greater Ways Publishing
PO Box 701017
St. Cloud, FL 34770
roofinflorida@aol.com
www.GregWooley.com

Disclaimer:

This collection of poems is meant to be inspirational in nature. The author of this book claims no religious training or affiliation with any particular form of religion. While the author hopes these poems might move the reader closer to a relationship with their Creator, he claims no special insight or power.

Permissions:

www.elenadudina.com (cover)
usabookcoach@gmail.com (cover and content coach)
www.facebook.com/DragonsChyldS (wizard)
ID: 592448684 quadshock/shutterstock.com
ID: 89356540 LilKar/shutterstock.com
ID: 85084930 cosma/shutterstock.com

Dedication

This book is dedicated to you Ronald.
Friends have come and friends have gone.
You knew a friend when you knew Ron.
Through the thin and through the thick
Ron kept his hand out to the sick
Over the years and without a pause
The sick and suffering were his cause
He'd share the tears and he'd share a laugh
A problem shared would be cut in half
He was responsible all the way to the end
It has been my privilege to call him friend
To a newcomer he'd never hesitate to give
some time and extend his hand
Love and tolerance ever the code when we
worked the steps as they're planned
So today I'm really happy... yet I'm really sad
You were the closest friend that so many had
Off to heaven and through the gate
To chair the big meeting you had a date

GEMS from G.O.D.

Our great loss is now heaven's gain
I'm so grateful your done with pain
I'm truly grateful for the time we shared
And to all the ones who know you cared
I say... Friends have come and Friends have gone
We're all so blessed to have known you Ron

Acknowledgments

I am so thankful to God for all the gifts in my life; this book would have never have happened without Him. I am specifically thankful for my wife Monica Wooley. Monica, you have been the greatest at supporting, encouraging and helping me to believe that I am and could be a writer. You always kept believing in me when I didn't believe in myself. I am so thankful I have the gift of these poems bouncing around in my head and for the poem that caught your eye Monica my love. I am grateful for the poem that started our adventure of a life together. I am so very thankful that ...*I wished on that star and had a word with the moon, that God would look down and have you come my way soon.* Who would have ever thought that a poem and a chat on America Online would have us together all these years later? My sweet Argentinian princess, I love you! Thank you for reading all of my poems over the years and for putting up with my daily "read this."

Kerissa, Kirsten, Sunjay and Duranne; my proof-reading team! You guys are absolutely awesome thank you so much for cleaning up my mess. Thank you for your visits when I was in the hospital. Sunjay you have great guitar skills and we rocked the hospital. If you didn't know, that first trip to the hospital was when I became committed to writing every day whether I felt like it or not. I thank you for all of your insights and your proofreading skills. Ladies thanks you for all the Christmas song parodies and silly rhymes we shared when you were little. I love you!

Luciano Svetlitze thank you for your encouragement and your inspiration. I am so proud of the man you've become. You are proof that hard work, dedication and discipline can make dreams come true. Watching you grow and transform has been a pleasure. You are an amazing son, brother and friend. I'm so glad you came into my life.

Alexander and Ezekiel Wooley thanks for your patience while I've been trying to finish this book.

Arron Rucker, Jason Line and Cindy Noel; my protection from the storm! You guys have made and continually make my life better. Without you guys in my life and your help to alleviate the crazies, I don't think this book would have ever happened.

Travis and Lizette Labell, and our Life Leadership family thank you for the support and inspiration.

Joe LaRosa at LaRosa Coaching thanks for the push to pursue my passions.

Contents

Introduction

Hello my broken friend, I've been waiting for you. Here's a little not-so secret, secret: I am broken too. So many times I have found myself sleepless in St. Cloud. Years ago, I could not sleep from the voices of self-hatred and anger shouting in my head. I did a lot of soul-searching and have healed a lot along the way. Prayer and meditation have brought new meaning in my life. Hope and healing that have come from a relationship with a Higher Power. I have learned to accept and love myself with all of the flaws that make me, me. Even the shiniest of gems are not without their flaws.

I have been in recovery from a hopeless state of mind. The way that I found hope was in and through a daily reprieve. I talk to God a lot and ask to be a better person than I was yesterday. Now, after many years of trying to repair the damage I did to myself as a younger man, I still find myself sleepless St. Cloud. It seems I'm meant to write poems in the middle of the night. It's not unusual for me lie awake at 3 am with a poem whispering to be written. I made reading something inspirational and writing a prayer, or a poem, part of my daily reprieve.

In this book, you'll see part of my poetic journey. I pray these poems help you love yourself as I have learned to love myself: as the flawed gems that we are. May they bring daily reprieve, rescuing you from a hopeless state of mind. May you Rise and Shine with a new hope for each day.

The Shiniest of Diamonds

The shiniest of diamonds come from the blackest of
coal
The wisest of wisdom comes from the most
damaged soul

So many times things are not just as they look
We can't judge the soup before it's had time to cook

Embracing your pains, your misery and your
brokenness
The transformation of your story is your chance to
bless

Going through hell doesn't mean that you're there to
stay
May every hurt be turned into compassion for
another on this very day

It takes time and severe pressure for a diamond to
transform
I pray you washed and made new at the end of the
storm

Something so hard yet so precious is transformed
from the blackest of coal
There are diamonds waiting to be uncovered from
every hurt in the depth of your soul

Our Most Valuable Asset

Some cherish their diamonds, others value their pearls

A country's most valuable asset is its young boys and girls

For what use is a full coin purse or a vault full of gold

If we're left without love when we're dying and old

Teach the children well and set them well on the way

To insure a brighter tomorrow and a much better today

When it comes down to it our greatest natural resource

Are our young men and women set well on their course

So take the time to teach and take the time to care

We are all on a journey a journey that we are meant to share

So for the sake of today and for the hopes of tomorrow

Help teach our young well and keep them from sorrow

More precious than diamonds, so much warmer than gold

Is a love that gives back when we've grown weary and old

Love Is

Love is our foundation, our walls and Love is our ceiling
Love is who we are, Love is so much more than a feeling

Love can make us cry and Love can call us to action
Love makes us shine a little brighter with the law of attraction

When you look into the mirror I pray you'd see a picture of Love
A living, loving, active image of our God above

Love is our foundation, our walls and Love is our floor
Love transforms the willing if we'll step through Love's door

The Cross Road

We stand at the cross road of hope and despair
When it comes to trouble we've all had our share

Narrow is the gate and straight is the way
I pray that you rise above the chaos on this very day

May you have one foot in heaven and one on the
earth
And dare to dig through your layers and discover
your worth

We are not what we've done and not what we did
Many go through a lifetime with their identity hid

Everything in this perishing world will come to a
loss
I pray the you discover your being at the heart of
the cross

May you be stripped clean to your own naked truth
And dream once again as in the days of your youth

Dream the dreams of who they told you should be
Dare to dream dreams of the joyous and free

So then at hope and despair you come to the center
The kingdom of God is waiting for you to come
enter

God's Gold

Value, oh value do you know what you're worth
God had you in mind from before your own birth

So much to learn, so much more to forget
Let's let the past be the past and let go of regret

Today is the day a great gift of the present
I won't be caught in replay with what I resent

I'll take charge of my mind and of my minds state
I'll act in positive action not relying on fate

I will take some moments to think and be still
And offer my life up to do my God's will

Do you know your own value, you are worth more
than gold

I pray you bring a smile to God's face when your
story is told

Value, oh value do you know what you're worth
God had you in mind before the day of your birth

Cause of Death

The number one cause of death has always been
birth
Do you let the temporary things of world give you
your worth

As we go about in pursuit of our why and the doing
our how
May you have the gift of the present and value the
now

If we really want to live then we must give our life
away
The real path to eternity is making the most of today

The number one cause of death has always been
birth
Our life is a gift of the Creator nothing can add or
take away from our worth

Real Eyes

Realize, real eyes help me to see
How I'm bound by selfishness and can't seem to
break free

I'm in my own way it seems I am my own storm
God free me from the bondage of self in its every
form

My ego is inflated and I'm all puffed up with selfish
pride
Then the voices of inferiority whisper your ego has
lied

The ride on the self centered cycle it baffles my
brains
I end back where I started bound by selfishness's
chains

Realize, real eyes help me to see
How I might think more of others and a little less of
me

Life Rope

God speaks to those who are longing to hear
Let me step into faith and step past my fear

Lord give me a vision that leads to a new road
The present has me weary, I need to help with my load

I long for Your Highways paved with purpose and hope
As You pull me ahead let me be Your life rope

A life rope to the hopeless and those that despair
I give my past, present and future into Your care
Every good blessing You give is a blessing to share

Greg Wooley

In Fear I Am

Inferior, in fear I am
Fear it acts like a big God dam

I can't move forward and I can't move back
How many times will fear get me off my track

I know it's illusion and it's not really real
Just how many dreams does come fear come to steal

It calls you less when you should be called more
It says don't knock when you stand at the door

The door of opportunity it stays closed tight
Every time we dare let fear win in faith's fight

I pray you'd dare to make courage your new friend
And the damn dam of fear would finally end

The river of the spirit then would start to flow
Then the adventures we'd have and places we could go!

Inferior, in fear I am not
In faithfulness my fear is forgot

Paths

Each and every day there are but two paths to take
We can choose selfishness or live for God's sake

Am I serving myself or in service to my Higher
Power
My ways bring loneliness, His bring joy unto my
last hour

There's something about us giving that it sets our
souls free
I pray I choose the path that lets me be all He'd
have me be

Living Water

You are the well from which living water can flow
God longs to use you but first you must start to
grow

Our secret sins and resentments are what sour the
well
When we could have a heavenly existence, we get
stuck in our own hell

A self-centered life never quite quenching our inner
thirst
We can't grasp our purpose and that seems like it's
the worst

I long to be more yet always I get in the way
Of doing everything God would have me doing on
this very day

You are the well from which living water can flow
Are you stuck in the past?...Well it's time you let go

Alone

An unfriendly person finds himself all alone
No one to share his burdens in life he's on his own

And the ungodly man will find himself thrown into
disgrace
With no one to share in the dreams that he longs to
chase

Senseless people will never walk the ways of those
that are wise
Forever concerned with how they look in each
other's eyes

The gossiper revealing, the comfort and peace his
words have stole
His slander and corruption penetrating to very
depths of his own soul

The spiritually hungry are humble and ever willing
to learn more
They are wide open, you will find that their heart is
an open door

(continued next page)

There is wellness and wisdom in the one who calls
God his friend
He makes messages from messes and sets things on
the mend

A friendly person is now and forever willing to
extend his hand
Walking towards the light and pulling others
towards all that God has planned

Cry Out

He gives power to the powerless and He gives
healing to the broken
Cry out in your need, miracles happen when our
prayers are spoken

All too often me and my ego, we get in God's way
I ask my Heavenly Father to make the most of me
everyday

Lord take all of my messes and these wars that I
wage
Help me to overcome so I can be Your message

You give me every breath that I take and You make
my heart beat
When I let You work in and through me I am whole
and complete

Lord You are my Creator I surrender to You
Point me in the direction to what You'd have me do

If You have a direction my answer is yes
I give me to You for those You might bless

You give power to the powerless and I'm thankful
for the broken that You heal
I am so grateful for my life and when You've shown
that Your miracles are real

Roof

From the depths of the gutter to top of the roof
That our God can transform I am living proof

Those chained by addiction, the spiritually
bankrupt, the mentally ill
The miraculous will and can happen if we would
give God our will

I thank God for Grace and for gifts that shouldn't be
I did everything wrong and He still rescued me

I am ever so grateful I'm drug free and there is no
drink in my hand
God I long to step fourth for all the dreams You
have planned

I shout from the top of the roofs free from the
gutters I once had to wallow
God has renewed and filled this heart that was so
empty and hollow.

Peace River

Peace is like a river that is ever on the flow
God can take our troubles but we must be willing to
let go

I wrestle and I war with issues I try to conquer on
my own
When I should be surrendering, laying my issues at
God's throne

God's peaceful rivers will take my issues off to sea
It's in and through surrender God makes the most of
me

Peace is like a river that's ever on the flow
I will plant myself beside it and God will help me
grow

Sower

The fields are fertile, there are seeds to be planted
Today is the day and I won't take it for granted

I will make a plan and I will stay the course
I will do the work and leave the rest to the Source

I gaze across the land and can't help see the needs
If there is to be growth we must first plant the seeds

If there is a need I am so much more than willing to
sow
If we are to have a great harvest we must be ready
to grow

The fields they are fertile, we're breaking new
ground
By our limiting beliefs… we will no longer be
bound

Our God gives the seeds and they need to be planted
Today is the day I pray we won't take it for granted

Heart of Stone

My heart of stone it has been replaced
I have new dreams for the old that I chased

Eyes off of me I would shift them to the Source
May we give God credit as we plot our course

There are two sides to most every coin
I long for a we that we can join

Not a me or a mine or a yours or a you
But something greater that Love flows through

A common bond with uncommon goals
Where we mend hearts and ignite souls

How I long to trade my me in for a we
And unite in purpose of setting people free

I pray that hearts of stone will be turned to flesh
And for the greater good our souls would mesh

Mark or Stain

Are we making our mark or just leaving a stain
Am I doing God's will or just living in vain

I've always worked hard let me start to work on
working smart
And release the champion I know God has instilled
inside my heart

How often our comfort zone becomes our self-
imposed cell
Kept us inside its walls by the self-limiting stories
we tell

Don't just leave a stain, dare to stand up and make
your mark
Success is just outside our comfort zone and it's
time we embark

Sink or Rise

We all will rise and we will all end up sinking
It starts and ends with the thoughts we're thinking

We end paying for the attention that we ourselves
have paid
What we focus on most is of what our foundation is
made

God gives us light and our thoughts they make the
shade
We will pay for the attention and for the attention
we've paid

When we wake in the morning and flip on the bad
news
What kind of focus is it that we are choosing to
choose

We will end up sinking or we will start to rise
It starts with what we hear and let into our eyes

Two Ended Candle

Are you leading life or is life leading you
To thine own self we should ever be true

So busy to and fro with no real meaning or
direction
No time to contemplate and no time for self
reflection

Never finding our why ...when we're so busy with
the how
How can we see tomorrow, when we're struggling
in the now

A two-ended burning candle will quickly burn out
its flame
A soul that never finds its purpose is a life that's
lost in shame

Are you leading your life or is your life leading you
I pray you find your God given purpose that sleeps
inside of you

Soil

God blesses the soil which is drinking up the rain
He makes us fertile in and through all of our living
pain

Today we cry and the tears they will surely flow
What we plant in our hearts are the seeds that will
grow

I pray you'll turn to the Lord for all your wants and
needs
May His words of Hope turn into sprouting planted
seeds

Each and every one of us we are our God's holy dirt
Transformation comes through our pain and our
hurt

God blesses the soil which is drinking up the rain
When the world's gone crazy I pray His love makes
you sane

Turning Point

It was at the turning point we came and we stood
God will make all things so they work for our good

Every time that we tumble, every time that we fall
God will one day use for foundation to help us grow
up and stand tall

When you come to the turning point don't you turn
and go back
A new freedom awaits us if we would just get on
the right track

Children of the EGO

Children of the ego; selfishness, anger and fear
I tried to have a look at me but I couldn't see me
clear

The defects of character tend to warp and they
cloud
Saying today I think I am humble and of that I am
proud

I hope and I pray one day this mess will come of
age
A balance between ego and humility and the war
they wage

The children of joy; happiness, contentment and
gratitude
God help clear my vision and give me a new
attitude

Denial Bound

The truth will set us free, a lie will keep us bound
In an honest self-appraisal, there is freedom to be
found

Denial keeps Life's river from flowing from its
Source
Self-deception like unseen sandbars that get me
stuck and throws me off course

Denial is a dam and the truth it lets us flow
God unclog the stream from you to me so I'll have
my chance to grow

Beyond our Circumstance

Father help us to step beyond our circumstance
And do some good when we have the chance

Our body's scarred and so is our soul
When we do Your will it makes us whole

In Your field of the spirit we reap and we sow
In the gift of giving is our chance to grow

Help us to fulfill the work that You would have us
do
When we see our reflection I pray we'd look like
You

Let us do some good when we have the chance
Sharing God's love moves us beyond our
circumstance

His Story, Her Story

His story, her story, my story and your story
Each and every one us has our own war story

Today is the day don't you dare to wait
Pull down those goals take them on a date

May today be the day you change the way you see
And step up to the plate and be all that you can be

His story, her story, my story and your story
Step forward and let your life bring God glory

Learn to Forget

So much to learn and yet so much more to forget
We did not come into this world with this shame
and regret

If my God can forgive me why in the world cannot
I
I'm letting go the old self so my old thinking might
die

It's time for all the old limbs to get a good and
healthy prune
In this learning and forgetting I will sing a brand-
new tune

So much to forget and there's always so much to
learn
Grace is our free gift it is not something we earn

Constructive Eyes

Accepting constructive criticism we take our place
among the wise
Alone in our own thinking we can't grow or open up
our eyes

In and through humility our path it will become
clear
God can and will grant wisdom when our heart is
sincere

Those who seek wise counsel have their seat among
the wise
How can we correct our course if we have
unopened eyes

Cream

It's always taken some churning to transform milk into cream
Don't you stop walking before you've stepped into your dream

I've done the math and you are adding up to awesome
Don't focus on the past or the troubles to come

It's often been said hardship is the path to peace
My burdens are gone when I let go, let God and release

The cream will rise but not before its taken its time to churn… . . . There's so much joy in this journey when we live and we learn

Lord Lord

Lord, Lord hear our prayer
All our lives are in Your care

Not to question but we come to ask
For this need as we do Your task

You care for the birds and the fishes in the sea
I know You're doing what You do in care for me

In your plans Father we will do our part
We love you God with our souls and heart

I pray for purpose, shelter, food and for rest
So today we would shine with all Your best

You shine today Lord and You'll shine some more
I ask You point my friends to the path and to the
door

To the door through which You would have them
grow and walk
So we could share Your truths and Your
foundational rock

Lord, Lord we would hear Your voice
To do Your will is our daily choice

Love and Lost

I loved and lost and lost a love
I give my thanks to God above

I can love and love and love again
I can love today and remember when

Remember when love wasn't and love was true
When Love becomes who we are, love's what we do

Grateful I'm not bitter from the bitter sweet
It's in and through God's love we're made complete

In love we win and in love we lose
To grow in love today is the choice I choose

Pain Into Gain

They say the Lord gives and the Lord takes away
It's in that giving and taking we're transformed
today

So often it's in loosing we find that we have gained
Would we choose growth if we've never been
pained?

It's in and by God's grace that I've lost and that I've
found
I ask for a new way of seeing so by the past I am
not bound

So often it's not what has happened but the way that
I see
That will or won't let me step forward to be all that
I can be

If I change my view there is a gift in most every
pain
When I walk with God He turns the loss into my
gain

Decisions, Decisions

Decisions, decisions I need to get in to action
When I get moving I invoke the law of attraction

Today is the day I will put out my hand
And help lift my brothers and sisters for all God has planned

A time for pondering, a time for prayer
A time for deep reflections and thoughts we might share

Decisions, decisions there's a time to decide
Then get into action and hold on for the ride

Children of the Light

We are called Children of Light; Christ's imitation
Let me live and love like Him; without limitation

Today's the day so shine and rise
Let me view others with His eyes

In His image I'm continually trying to be
He gave me Grace and Grace set me free

Bridge of Love

Bridge builder, bridge builder today is the day
If this world is going to change we need to show
them the way

The way to loving God, our enemy, our neighbor
and friend
And then we'll love for the earth so this world it
might mend

Bridge builder, bridge builder bridging from the
past and into tomorrow
Today Love is the bridge that crosses over this
worlds anger and sorrow

Rest

I pray you comfort, I pray you blessed
When life brings its troubles, I pray you rest

When the morning comes and you face the day
I pray God fills you with sunshine when the skies
are gray

I pray you a calmness and I pray you a healing
Most of all I pray God give strength in whatever
you're dealing

Shaking the Salt

Even the salt of the earth at times needs a good
shake
To remind us of the difference that we're here to
make

You are a light to the world so take off that shade
Stand tall and shine on the foundation that our God
has laid

It's time to remember that we're here to be salt to
this earth
You are uniquely designed and your life story has
worth

So give your testimony and give this world a good
shake
There is difference out there that you're meant to
make

Living to Serve

Living to serve while serving to live
There are gifts inside of you that you're meant to
give

We waste so much time being anxious and nervous
And we let so many moments go by where we could
be of service

Of service to God and of service to our fellow man
Possessed by our possessions was never part of the
plan

Giving to gain while gaining to give
It's through letting go that we're learning to live

Holier Than Thou

I longed that I might be holy, not just holier than
thou
So God might really use me in some way or some
how

Holy's definition says that we are belonging and
that we are a part
Prayer was the gateway that opened up the doorway
into my heart

I longed that we might be holy, not just holier than
others
If we really knew God we would all be sisters and
brothers

Weep the People

Weep the people it seems so sad
What happened to the US that we once had

We have become a nation of the entertained
Our moral fabric becoming torn and stained

Our heroes are like the gladiators of yesteryear
I can't help but notice the lack of Romans here

Lady Liberty she surely sheds some tears
As we become the land of hate and fears

She stands in the harbor torch growing dim
Our self-centered eyes have lost sight of Him

In God we trust is now the land of love of money
God shakes His head but there is nothing funny

The great melting pot has become a great divided
land
This cannot be the vision of freedom our forefathers
planned

Freedom from has replaced what was once the
freedom of
Our land was the beacon and the light of God's love

Weep the people it seems so sad
Where's the US that we once had

Free From

Free from fear and free from worry
Free from burdens, no need to hurry

You are a miracle just in case you didn't know
Every pain is a dose of spiritual miracle grow

So let me not ask today that I would be pain free
Let me embrace that pain to make the most out of
me

In pain's embrace I lose my worry and I lose my
fear
My eyes open to the miracle of the one in the mirror

My eyes are open and I can clearly see
The miracle you are and you're meant to be

Free from worry and freedom from fear
Setting people free is why we are here

What's Your Charge

Every person a prisoner within their own cell
With God as our center, we are worthy and well

He is our nucleus and we are His charge
I am quite positive He wants us living large

He is the Dream Weaver and we are His threads
The gifts He has given shouldn't go to our heads

Today I will step fourth knowing I am made for His
Glory
May we hear well done faithful servant at the end of
our story

Every person is a prisoner within their own head
Our cellular charge is in the food our spirit is fed

Wake up Dreamer

Come now dreamer it is time that we wake
There is a work to be done and a difference to make

We all have our gifts and our talents we are meant
to use
To bring hope to the hopeless and share the Good
News

God gave you vision and I hope that you see
There are so many in bondage that long to be free

We can use our hurt and our healing the gift of our
story
To take the eyes off the suffering to bring our God
glory

Come now dreamer there is no time to sleep
God has gave us promises I know that He'll keep

The Source and the Flow

I look to the Source and I step into the Flow
If I am going to move forward I have to let go

Let go of the past and let go of the fear
Let go of what was and get really clear

Clear on my goals and clear on my part
If I don't know where I'm going how can I start

Start on the journey that makes the most out of me
If I can break my own chains I might set people free

Today is the day and I will truly give it my best
When we give what we've gained is when we
become blessed

I look to the Source and I step into the Flow
If we are going to move forward we have to Let Go

I Know You

Child of God so very different yet quite the same
I think that I know you but perhaps not your name

They've tried to label, some good and some bad
They're ever changing with the current day's fad

Child of God; you bright shining soul
You need no label to make you whole

Tucked Away Blessings

My blessings are counted and I tuck them away
I keep them close to remind me if my day goes
astray

To remind me of the gifts that I have and the gifts
that I've had
If I just attempt to be grateful I cannot walk around
mad

The things we love get lost when we take them for
granted
I pray you start your day with the seeds of gratitude
planted

My blessings are counted one, two and three
Better than perfect I'm the me God-meant me to be

Stuck in a Rut

A rut is like a coffin with the ends that we've kicked
out
So many times we're stuck and we're dying to get
out

My every day routines they set me on my route
Things they need to change that I cannot dispute

It's the little daily habits that help set us on our way
Do I count my blessings, make time to pray every
day

Take some time to read and make sure my mind is
fed
Ask someone for guidance and become willing to
be led

A rut is like a coffin and I'm unwilling to be stuck
To overcome insanity it takes much more than luck

God's Vine

My spirit is shining, my hopes they are high
I know the Way and I know my Why

There is so much in this life that we are meant to be
Our dreams are slowly die when we are not living
free

A slave to my old thinking, my past and enslaved to
my debt
We don't have to wallow in the cesspool of remorse
and regret

Our minds are like a vibrant springs that we need to
keep flowing
When we learn and then we teach it ensures that we
are growing

My Hopes they are sky high giving my spirit a
brand new shine
A life with passion and purpose is the sweetest fruit
on God's vine

Teaching to Learn

Teaching and learning and learning and teaching
Humility keeps us relatable to those we are
reaching

I pray that we don't look down on anyone without
the desire to lift
Learning the art of giving and receiving is truly a
God given gift

In life we learn what we should do and what we
should not
We can learn something from everyone should not
be forgot

Teaching to learn and learning to teach
People are waiting that you are meant to reach

God's Gift

God's gift is new life and setting us on the Way
Our job is to acceptance and to make the most of
the day

He made us on purpose and we didn't happen by
chance
He's willing and wanting to move us beyond
circumstance

We move beyond luck when He calls us His blessed
We can't out give the Giver in this He invites us to
test

God's gift is new life and we can accept it today
Lord grow our hearts as we walk in Your way

Truth in Love

For the love of truth, there is truth in Love
I long to be filled with the wisdom of God up above

This world it whispers half truths and shouts out its lies
I long to live Love's commandment and be love in God's eyes

When we love the law and forget the law of love
We'll find that we've drifted from our God above

We are commanded to love God and our neighbors as ourselves; no law more important than these
I pray I might live out this command each and every time that I hit my knees

There is truth in Love and I know it to be fact
Today may the love of truth cause you step forth and to act

Greg Wooley

A Loving Relief

A love without condition, a love beyond belief
A love that doesn't burden simply brings relief

A relief from the self torment, a relief from this
worldly pain
A relief from the self destruction that truly is insane

A love that brings meaning to meaninglessness
when all this life seems for naught
A love that sees my shortcomings, identifies them,
transforms them, then they are forgot

A love that kept a calling in and through my darkest
time
A love that didn't care if I had a dollar, a penny or a
dime

That's the Love I found when my knees they finally
hit the floor
That's the Love that Christ has waiting if we'll
knock upon the door

Hunger

I hunger for truth and I thirst in my spirit
Lord you hold wisdom and I long to hear it

Father time and time again you have inspired and
still I am left longing for more
You hold the key to transformation I pray You
would unlock the door

You take the worst and You bring out the best
The morally bankrupt You turn into the blessed

The most broke of the broken You make better than
new
I ask You to take my broken pieces and make me
like You

Not so I might boast but that I might truly live
I give thanks to You for the gifts You gave so I
could give

There is nothing in this life can we truly call our
own
For today and for forever I am thankful for the gifts
that you loan

To discover new truths I am so very eager in heart
God you are the holder of eternity and You are
where wisdom does start

I Close My Eyes

I close my eyes and I pray I might see
A vision of the person I'm meant to be

The past is the past and today I'll leave it behind
And do what I must to renew my heart and my mind

Life is a game where we give and receive
Our limitations are in what we choose to believe

Today I believe all things are possible and I pray
that you do too
Choose well what goes in the heart and the mind so
that He can renew

Fate

Today is the day, I'm not willing to wait
I'll get into action, I won't wait upon fate

With a plan and a goal I will act and adjust
I'll step and step forward with people I know like
and trust

With God given purpose let's live out the dream
So many lives will be changed as we're moving
ahead full steam

Today is the day to wait I'm not willing
Lord let me shine with Your light and the hope
You're instilling

Team

I pray you blessed, I pray for our team
I pray we get running, chasing our dream

May the blessed get to blessing and give all we can
give
And offer hope to the hopeless by the Life that we
live

I'm not going to wait, today is the day
Our dreams are a waiting lets get on the way

Today is the day let's dare take a stand
And live in the abundance that our God has
planned

I pray for our team and I pray you blessed
I pray that we would be sharpened into our very
best

Fear's Web

Fear and shame are like a web with so many an
unseen strand
Keeping us from stepping forward to all that God
has planned

Fear is ever pulling us back in to our suffer rings
Afraid of the very day and what tomorrow brings

I went to my Creator and He whispered Love is my
name
His love became a fire, burning away my fear and
my shame

Then His love then became my new web with so
many an unseen strand
Attaching to every nerve in me guiding me towards
all that He has planned

He has me polishing up my talents and He's giving
even more
So I might shine all the brighter and lead others to
Hope's door

Lost and Loved

I loved and lost and lost a love
I give my thanks to God above

I can love and love and love again
I can love today and remember when

Remember when love wasn't and love was true
When Love becomes who we are, love's what we do

Grateful I'm not bitter from the bitter sweet
It's in and through God's love we're made complete

In love we win and in love we lose
To grow in love today, it's love I choose

Thanksgiving

Thankful for the sunshine and thankful for the rain
Thankful for the pleasure and thankful for the pain

Thankful for when I receive and so thankful when I
give
I pray I would be thankful for my breath and
everyday I live

Life is the true gift we so often take for granted
Gratitude will grow when thankfulness is planted

So take a little chance on this Thanksgiving day
To stop and count your blessings and to bless some
on the way

I am thankful for you friend, I pray you a grateful
heart
When we go looking for a great day gratitude is it's
start

Legacy

Each and every life a stone thrown in life's legacy
Our choices making waves that come from you and
me

It's the little daily habits, we have to choose with
care
They make our lives worth living and determine
what we'll share

What we'll share with our children and our children
that are grand
A person without long term vision leads a life that
goes unplanned

Each and every life a precious stone, you are not
here by chance
Dare to dream of more and move beyond your
circumstance

I pray you make some waves and leave a legacy
And dare to shine your light for all the world to see

Field of Dreams

I went out a roaming in the field of dreams
Nothing in this life is really what it seems

So often our belief is what does and doesn't make
things so
I pray that I would become a master in the art of
letting go

Self-esteem, self-doubt and self-deception they ever
hold us back
I will let go of self and serve as a messenger rolling
along God's track

Out in the field of dreams, I am a planter of dream
seeds
Faith without works is dead I pray I plant hope
through my daily deeds

Island

When each of us is an island in a ocean of despair
When waves of trouble come it's trouble we all
share

We act like we're not connected and ignore each
other's pain
Everyone one of us a child of the Creator; yet we
live our lives in vain

We act like we're not connected and ignore each
other's pain
Taking humaneness from humanity is what's
driving us insane

Societal desperation has but one immunity
Hope comes alive within us with unity of
community

Not one of us is then an island if we all become the
sea
When hope is on the rise it lifts both you and me
When none of us is then an island we can become a
tranquil sea

What Are You Thinking

What are you thinking it seems perhaps that you
forgot
That every good action starts out with just a
thought

What we put in our mind is a daily choice that we
choose
We can create our own destiny that's both good and
bad news

So many of us don't take time to think that what
we're thinking is a primary chore
If we are to have a chance at a better tomorrow our
mind becomes the door

They say that if we can think it, then we actually
might
But if we think that we can't then we're probably
right

What are you thinking... I pray that it's Good News
All of our actions come from the thoughts that we
choose to choose

Mountains will move for those with the faith to
believe that they can
I pray that today by that the renewing of my mind
I'll be that kind of man

I Have My Why

I have my reason and I have my why
I'm spreading my wings, I'm ready to fly

When I look in to me and my legacy
I pray I'd be a vehicle to set people free

Free from the fear, freedom from debt
Free to live passionately and leave go of regret

They say that hurt people hurt people, I know that
the healed they can heal
I long to help others live out the meaning and
purpose they're meant to feel

So I'm diving in deep into my legacy
Lord let me help others be all they can be

So Many Talking

So many of us talking with so little to say
I pray I might say something of real value today

Much more than the squeaking of an old rusty
wheel
Something to inspire that might change how we feel

Words have real power they can hurt, they can help,
they can heal
Do my words lift up others or do they degrade and
they steal

So many of us talking with so little to say
I pray I would have some discernment when my
mouth opens today

Human

We are called human being not human been
So many of us can't live in the moment we're in

In fear of the future by the past we are pained
We could be renewed yet so many are stained

I will open my hands, not hold on too tight
It's in letting go that today is made right

We are called human beings so for today I'll just be
It's when we live in the moment we become truly
free

His Art

A sculptor needs to chip away, a painter needs to
brush
You are the good Lord's work of art, He's seldom in
a rush

All our fears and failures, all our brokenness and
pain
He uses to draw us closer to Him, so they never are
in vain

A painter needs to brush and a sculptor chips away
I'm letting go over everything to be His masterpiece
today

Stones In A Pond

Our lives are like stones thrown into a pond
The waves of our actions can go so far beyond

Before I take action let me take time to reflect
Just how and who my actions might come to effect

At least once in my life time I hope my life's stone
might cause a great wave
And bring a ripple of hope to those that addiction
and pain would enslave

Uphill

As I step into His will let me walk in the way
Help me learn from the past yet live in today

Everything worthwhile in this life comes from an
uphill climb
I pray for wisdom and discernment to make the
most of my time

Lord let me be more than I was and move beyond
circumstance
I'm grateful for the gift of this life and my second
chance

As I step in Your will let me walk in the way
I give thanks that my mess is a message today

He the Sea

If I were a river and He were the Sea
I'd give Him my all, He'd give all to me

I would return to Him no matter the plot or the
plight of my course
He would be with me through drought and through
flood for He is my Source

There are parts of me shallow and there are parts of
me deep
In the endless giving and taking there is so much to
reap

My waters they are muddy and my waters they are
clear
I will always have safe passage if I would just let
Him steer

He is with me through spring time, summer, winter
and fall
The flow between us is established when I surrender
and call

He is the Sea and I am His river
Every good gift given is returned when it's gave for
the Giver

Stumbler

Many times I have stumbled and many times I have fell
Many times my poor choices have made my life a living hell

Failing doesn't make failures as long as we're willing to rise
Success is in the making when the fallen gets up and tries

Today is the day let me dare to try something new
Help me to live and keep learning in everything I do

Every time that we've stumbled, every time that we've fell
Are little pieces of wisdom in the stories that we tell

Time

Time and time and time again
We put off dreams til someday when

Tomorrow's coming is no guarantee
Today I pray to make the most of me

Cut the anchors and spread your wings
Live what if and what it brings

Time and time and time again
Today's the day for someday when…

The Plain

Off of the path and on to the plain
Many get glimpses few can remain

It's not what we know but what we know not
It seems once could see but it seems we forgot

There's so much we can know yet more to forget
In the moment I can lose my self; my pain and my regret

Off of the path and on to the spiritual plain
The ways of this world leave few of us sane

Plight

Growing or recessing ever seems the plight
As for me my friend I will shine with the light

Shine the light of freedom, shine the light of hope
And to the downtrodden I will offer God's life rope!

Punch A Hole

Follow your dreams, punch a big hole in the sky
The Universe responds when we have a goal and a why

The impossible becomes possible when we truly believe
Combining courage and faith is when we truly achieve

The Greatest Invention

You and I have in us the greatest intentions
We are the Creators most creative inventions

In our minds what we dare to dream We can
manifest
Miracles and wonders come about when We think
the best

It's all in your mind I pray that you see
What we dare to think about is what we will be

Nourish the Child

I pray you nourish the child inside
All those hurts we don't need to hide

A childhood lost can be born anew
Take time to nourish the child in you

A hurt in the light can start to heal
So many of us know just how you feel

There'll be scars we all know it's true
Take time to nourish the child in you

Yesterday's gone tomorrow's not here
In the present there is nothing and nothing here to
fear

The child in me cries when you cry too
Time to nourish the child that's inside of you

Planting and Reaping

Sowing and reaping, reaping and sowing
What we are planting is what we are growing

How much we are giving decides on what we'll
receive
How much would I give if I had real faith to really
believe

Money is a tool meant for the fulfillment of needs
I pray I would use it wisely in all of my deeds

Everything in this world is but a gift and a loan
I can't even decide to take one breath on my own

Today is a day I'll gratefully give and receive
God you bring new hope to those that believe

Fruit on the Limb

There is a life fact that we really can not dispute
That we judge and are judged by our life's fruit

When you look at me I pray you see on every limb
Leaves and fruit that would remind you of Him

Lord let me drink from your well and bear the fruit
of the spirit
I look to You for Your wisdom, how my soul longs
to hear it

Leading Astray

Are you leading the way or are you leading astray
Where would we go if I went with you today

If I did what you did and have done what you've
done
Would it benefit others with the prize we had won

God I pray everything I do would lead to you as the
Source
I hope I inspire others to walk with me as You're
plotting my course

God I've seen You take the broken and You call
them blessed
Today let me take step another towards You and
give You my best

Every one of us a leader, with today a new chance
to lead
When we find a way to go together we all can
succeed

Leading astray or leading the way
May your actions and your deeds be worth
following today

Gifts

And as far as gifts go I thought this the worst
Far from being grateful it seemed I was cursed

The blue lights they flashed as I looked back in my
mirror
My heart it stopped dead and I was quite filled with
fear

I had been here before now I was here once again
There was a lesson to be learned I just didn't know
when

It seemed I was always dead drunk and that dead
drunk I would die
The best and worst gift I ever received came in the
form of a D U I

Several thousands in fines and sometime in the cell
Was but the beginning of the end of my self-
imposed hell

As we head for the bottom each one has to hit rock
God gives power to the powerless as we start this
new walk

(cOntnued next page)

One day at a time we start trudging the pathway to peace

Giving our will over to God, from selfishness finding release

For most every one of us there's a moment we're brought to our knees
In desperation we cry out to God and He does hear our pleas

Perhaps for you it's not a drug and it's not a drink
But it's way that you see things or the broke way you think

All too often the worst gifts ever they can turn in to the best
From being sure that we're cursed, we become grateful and blessed

Choosing

When choosing your choices I pray you choose
wise
My you envision your greatness when closing your
eyes

May you dream a great dream of all you can be
Of all the lives we can change when we're truly free

There are great things to be done when we find our
tribe of like mind
New dreams and new visions come to the eyes that
were blind

I've left someday aisle, let's get on the way
There is a difference to be made let's make it today

Alive and Aware

Visualize, visualize I pray and I see
All that I am and that I am meant to be

There are times we should follow and times we should lead
Our relationships are crucial if we are to succeed

In the book of life tomorrow's pages are blanks
There's a difference we can make together for that I give my thanks

When I close my eyes I become alive and aware
Of the gift of life and life's gifts we're meant to share

Keepers of The Earth

Children of God; Keepers of the Earth
Loving each other, knowing your worth

Every day is a new chance, I pray that it'd be
A picture of Love placed in your memory

Take time to take time and get you some rest
Commune with the Creator and know that you're
blessed

You have but one life and one life to live
May you reflect on the blessings that you're meant
to give

Then give of the heart and share the gifts of your
spirit
There is a message in you and this world longs to
hear it

Children of God I pray you would remember your
worth
God had you in mind before the day of your birth

And if you are the hurting I pray that you heal
May Love make you new and start to reveal

Reveal that you are a Child of the Creator a Keeper
of Earth
It's in loving God and each other that we find our
worth

The Great Divide

I looked out across our world's great divide
Wondering how it ever, ever grew so very wide

The democrat, the republican, the red, the blue, the white and the black
Our babies never do get to choose their side of the track

The democrat, the republican, the red, the blue, the white and the black
Our God is calling...Now let's call Him back

If we stand for nothing we surely will fall
Our God is calling and I'm taking that call

If we stand for nothing then one day nothing will stand
I ask that we would stand for God and His great command

I stand for love and I love you my friend
And I believe that in Love this world it can mend

The rich, the poor, the black and the white
Each and every one of us is made for our God's delight

I look to the great divide and I pray it filled with great Love
We are all made in the image of Christ and our God up above

A Time to Polish

There is a time to polish and there is a time to shine
I walk in the way of the One who turned water to wine

He is the Alpha and the Omega, the Beginning and End
I call him my Teacher and Master and He calls me His friend

He turns trash in to treasure and He's making the old into new
He's willing and waiting to work wonders through me and through you

There was a season to polish, it's come time that we shined
He is removing the scales and giving new sight to the blind

God's giving a 2020 vision of a new shining season
The hopeless now have hope and Christ is the reason

Grateful for...

I'm grateful to sleep and I'm grateful to wake
Grateful for my gifts and the difference I make

Grateful for my children and grateful for my wife
Grateful for the chances that God gives in this life

With an attitude of gratitude I am starting this day
I pray that I would have the to courage to encourage
with every word that I say

I am grateful to wake and I am grateful to rest
I am grateful for Life, I am so very blessed

Flooded Wisdom

May you be flooded with wisdom until you
overflow
Step out of your comfort zone to help others to
grow

I pray love and tolerance would become more than
a code
As we step fourth and help the burdened to carry
their load

I am letting wisdom, love and tolerance become my
life's way
I ask God to use and make the most of me on this
very day

Give

Give a person a fish and he will eat for the day
Yet that person's world will change if we would
show them the way

Shown the way that he might be involved in
changing his mind
And his eyes might open into the ways he once was
blind

You can lead a horse to water but you can't make
him drink
For my life to really change I had to change what I
think

Life is ever changing if we're to live we're to grow
Lord let me be open to learn everywhere that I go

So when I come upon new waters let me take a deep
drink
And be open to information that might change how
I think

Fulfilled

So many aren't fulfilled because they are never
filled full
We get to running on empty because we can't find
the tool

The tool to help us change to let us be all we might
be
We get stuck in the past and can't seem to break free

Our daily habits our instrumental if we are to refill
Let me take time for something positive, a time to
be still

Lord help me be fulfilled because you've filled me
full
Every day help me grow sharper as You make me
Your tool

Worrier to Warrior

From a worrier to a warrior, trade that O for an A
I am living out the change I want to see every day

No matter what happens, don't just leave it to fate
I am in control of my thinking, I will take charge of
my state

Transformation happens in the here and the now
When we know our why, God will give us the how

I am so very blessed; I pray I would be used as a
blessing
I've traded my O for an A and today I'm not
stressing

From a worrier to a warrior, I will get in to motion
To live out my higher calling I will give my
devotion

Start with Me

I find there is a little bit more peace on earth
When I embrace self-love and feel self-worth

If the world is to change let it start with me
Let me live out the difference I long to see

Self-acceptance and self-love are the keys to self-caring
They bring greater depth and worth to all that we're sharing

The truest life love affair begins with the one in the mirror
We can't be of maximum service to others until we have that clear

I find my balance and I find peace on this earth
When I embrace self-love and know my self-worth

Feelings are Feelings

Feelings are feelings; they are meant to be felt
Truth is the truth it's best when its properly dealt

Take time to embrace pain as if it were an old
friend
Then send pain on its way and take time to mend

The pains in our memories are but tricks of the
mind
If we'd just drop the rocks there is freedom to find

A hurt overcome can become like a brand new key
One to open the door and set a fellow sufferer free

Feelings are feelings they're neither good nor are
they bad
How much joy we could feel if we felt every feeling
we've had

Freely

Freely He gives so we can freely receive
So many gifts for those that truly believe

Starting with Grace that renews and fuels us with
Love
So many are the promises when walk with our God
above

He gives strength to the weary and He empowers
the weak
He is the bringer of wisdom to the words which we
speak

As I move closer to God, He moves closer to me
I gave Him my will and then He set me free

So today I receive what my Savior He freely gave
By grace I was saved and I'm no longer a slave

Resentment

Resentment a poison that we choose to drink
Corrupting our souls and the thoughts that we think

Our souls they shine when we live and let live
I get forgiveness when I learn how to forgive

Forgiveness and trust they are not one and the same
And in forgiving there's not restoration in
forgiveness's claim

It's by forgiving I'm taking back the way that I feel
The old wound may hurt but it's starting to heal

Resentment is a poison I no longer thirst
By a lifetime of hurts I refuse to be cursed

Seeds and Weeds

Seeds of greatness and weeds of doubt
Every garden has weeds that we need to pull out

The mind is our garden on which we focus will flourish
By our daily habits we grow what we nourish

Take care in your associations, guard what you see
Constant negative news, won't help you be all you can be

The seeds are there they have already been planted
Only you dream your dreams don't take them for granted

A dream with a date turns into a goal
Chasing our dreams inspires our soul

Seeds of greatness and weeds of self-doubt
Having an abundant garden is what life's all about

Unity

Unity of community; united in life and the way that
we walk
May our God's love shine through in every word
that we talk

There are times we should lead and there are times
we should follow
And if we are to keep peace sometimes it's our pride
we must swallow

There are so many gifts to make use of and discern
When to shine and to shade I pray the courage to
learn

When Love is loving that love is not out to offend
We can show off His great work when we've made
a new friend

There's unity in community come we invite you
along
In Love's transformation right can come from most
every wrong

Find a Need

Shake a hand and plant a seed
Make a friend and find a need

A time to reap and a time to sow
What we plant is what will grow

If we put anger out we get anger back
A kind word can change our track

Change the track of the way we're living
In this life we always get what we're giving

Plant a seed with a hug and a hand shake
Today I will live the difference I long to make

Humble Pie

Let me start the day with a slice of humble pie
God you give me wisdom and my reason why

You give me breath and you make my heart beat
When I am close to You Father I feel I'm complete

All too often my pride and ego get in the way
I'll have a slice of humble to start out the day

All the Air

All the air that we breathe, every thought that we
think
All of the food that eat and every drop that we drink

Father you know and provide for all of my needs
I pray I might bring you glory with my words and
my deeds

When we're walking in faith we have no need to
worry
Father with You the race is won I don't have to
hurry

From the water we drink and to the air that we
breathe
Lord you are the giver of every good gift for those
that believe

Master's Key

In a world full of locked hearts Lord make me Your
key
Today there are so many slaves that need to be free

Bound by our habits in a world full of distraction
Father if you point the way I will step into action

I offer You my will let me walk in Your way
God fill me with words that You'd have me say

I thank You for breaking my chains link after link
You are renewing my heart, transforming the way
that I think

God I give my praise, You are my victory
In a world full of locks You are the Master Key

Turn the Page

Life chapters they will end and the new pages get
turned
What will you write next now that you've lived and
you've learned

I pray that you live with a purpose and try
something new
While your living out the story that's making you,
you

For a better chapter to get started in your life's
letter
We must want to do something to make ourselves
better

To learn something once and repeat for the next
thirty years
It makes for a sad story and it should bring you to
tears

Life's for the living and those of us that are living
we grow
No matter how much we know there's much more
we can know

Life chapters they end and one day when your
pages get read
I pray it's a story of a full life and of a mind and of a
spirit that got fully fed

Prayer-orities

I pray for serenity and a sober state of mind
I pray every day I might be just a little bit more kind
I pray for my family, my fellowship, my church and my friends
I pray when I'm wrong for the humility to make an amends
I pray I would live by Godly principles and live out His plan
I pray everyday I would seek out inspiration to be a decent man
I pray I leave the past in the past and live today like its brand new
These are some of my prayer-orities, what about you?

Nature and Nurture

It takes nature and nurture to achieve restoration
We need a quiet place for a deep soul exploration

How deep do you go when you go diving into your
legacy
There are so many self-imposed slaves that need to
be free

Modern day slavery's chains they come with so
many a link
So many of us make our own shackles by the way
that we think

It takes both nature and nurture to truly achieve
Don't let the status quo tell you what to believe

Angels Whisper

When angels come whisper what do you hear
Are they sweet words of joy or harsh words of fear

Some murmur of trembling and a great gnashing of
teeth
Yet others whisper the of love of God as the
universal belief

When God whispers to me I hear hope and ways to
restore
I step toward the light so I don't have to hurt any
more

I pray that I might be a reflection; a little piece of a
God mirror
That I would be used to bring hope to any and all
that would hear

When Angels come whisper I pray that they bring
Your reason to dance and your reason to sing

Gifts

All of us have gifts in which we are entrusted
Often they go unused and they end up all rusted

It's not what we don't have but it has always been
what we do
That's making the most out of me and will make the
most of you

I get caught up in thoughts of what I'm not and I
start comparing
Instead of polishing the gifts I have and that I could
be sharing

All of us have gifts within us we are meant to use
Talents shined or tarnished is our choice to choose

Greg Wooley

Not the Fair

This is life and it's not the fair
Pain is something that we all share

I start to blame and call it a curse
In my sorrows my pain is worse

On that which I focus it seems to grow
So I embraced the pain then let it go

Today is the day the pain is not here
It is my focus that keeps pain near

Misery is optional pain is sure
How I see things is the cure

Cry from yesterday or dread tomorrow
The pain is not here yet still I sorrow

What should be's and remember when's
Today is the day I will choose my lens

I will choose to see life much as the fair
With wonders to behold most everywhere

Life often gives us what we choose to see
On what I am choosing to focus is up to me

Meditation

Worry is like meditation that looks for the answers in me
Like the same thinking that created the issues will set me free

Let me not worry for a moment, a minute or one precious hour
Help me to think about God and His principles to transform and empower

Foundations

The pains we've felt and the mistakes we've made
Become the rocks in the concrete when our
foundation is laid

We fall and we stand and we stand and we fall
Often it's in our pain when we cry out and call

Call out to God as He comes takes our right hand
He was calling us also for all that He has planned

May I become willing to change, willing to open
my heart and willing to open my ears
I pray God use all of my pain and give me the
courage to overcome all of my fears

The mistakes that I have made and the pains that I
have felt
Become the rocks in my foundation when I've
overcome, accepted and dealt

Pride

Pride slams the door, humility eases it open
I need to be teachable if I want to leave hope in

All to often our own best thinking is a dead end
street
And our pride leaves us separated and alone in our
defeat

Sometimes we need shut our mouths and open our
eyes
Being willing to seek outside counsel is the way of
the wise

Greg Wooley

Friends

Friends of old and friends of new
I count my blessings for friends like you

We shared some laughter, we've shared some pain
You're more cherished than words can explain

You gave your time and you gave a hand
You picked me up when things weren't as planned

Friends like you never thought to count the cost
You helped me find the real me when I was lost

Friends of old and friends of new
When I think of friends I think of you

The Great Deceiver

The greatest deceiver of me has always been me
There is so much about me I can't even see

I pray today that when I look at myself in the
mirror
That who I am and who I'm meant to be would be
crystal clear

Take away my denial and let me see through the
blame
If the truth can set one free then it's freedom I shall
claim

Lord give me eyes to see through my self-
deception
My biggest road blocks today are me and my
perception

Every Day Gift

Lord, Lord, hear my prayer
Life's a gift we're meant to share

We arrive with nothing and we leave the same way
Let me make the most of my gifts every day

There's not much more that makes us feel alive or
helps us to live
Than when we are giving away the gifts God meant
us to give

Lord, Lord, hear my prayer
Life's a gift we're meant to share

Our Words

Our words they can hurt, our words they can heal
Have a care with your words no matter how you
might feel

Once off of the tongue we can't take them back
How many times do careless words knock our lives
right off the track

Let me be quick to listen and slow when I speak
Lord help me control my tongue when I'm feeling
weak

Clarity

Clarity, oh clarity we need get clear
If we don't know where we're going we're already
here

A people with no vision they surely will die
In order to thrive we need a dream and a why

A building with no blueprint or plan will never get
built
A soul with no hope for the future can't help but
wilt

Clarity, oh clarity I need to get clear
To serve a purpose greater than me is why I am here

Perfect Imperfection

Perfect imperfection so much like a wave
So it is with the gift of our humanness the Creator
gave

Each and every one us different yet we are quite the
same
Yet ego and pride so often revoke that God given
the claim

As waves go in and out we are born and we die
So few of us dive in to the depths of our mysterious
why

Perfect imperfection so much like a wave
I pray you the pursuit of your God given passions
until you go to the grave

Come now Sleeper

Come now sleepers it's time that we wake
There are lives to transform; a difference to make

The ant and the elephant are becoming one mind
God, man and earth desperately need realigned

To be aligned as in the olden when the one was for
three and the three were for one
I pray we realize that we are all connected before
mankind is completely undone

We talk about vision, purpose and of our self worth
Truly, where is our value when we're killing the
earth

We claim to know the Father while the Mother we
bleed
How can this disregard for Creation expect to
succeed

Man cared for earth and the earth cared for man
Such was the covenant before we twisted the plan

Come now sleepers it's time that we rise
A true heaven on earth I long for that prize

Every When

Every when and everywhere
I look for God and find Him there

In the mountains and by the sea
He's in the very heart of me

We find Him when we truly seek
I pray He is in every word I speak

Everywhere and every when
I looked and looked and then looked again

In the mountains and by the sea
God is alive in the heart of me

Faith By

Faith it comes by hearing and strength comes by
doing
It is by our daily habits that our souls they get
renewing

Exercise the body and read some food for thought
Take time to pray and meditate so God won't be
forgot

Excellence doesn't happen by luck or just by chance
It's the choices I choose today that make my
circumstance

Faith comes by hearing, we gain strength when it's
done
It's in our daily habits the game of life is lost or won

A Live One

In walking the paths least likely to resist
Just how many wonders have we missed

In this life there are so many obstacles to overcome
and mountains we can climb
I pray that I choose a path on growth's mountain
and to make the most of my time

For any dead fish can float down stream
But it takes a live one to chase the dream

Lord lead me to the paths that You would have me
go
Help me to overcome every obstacle that would let
me grow

A Loose Fitting Shirt

We need to wear this world like a loose fitting shirt
So we can shake off its troubles and shake off its
hurt

When the shirt gets to many stains that shirt it gets
tossed
We begin to think of ourselves as dirty and our
identity gets lost

You my friend are not and have never been the shirt
that you wear
When our God washes us clean those stains are no
longer there

Today is the day to live our life as a new creation
Jesus arms are open and giving us His invitation

Then we can all wear shirts that are made of Light
Claim your identity friend you are our God's delight

Hidden Treasure

In your heart is a hidden treasure
Beyond the pain, beyond the pleasure

Clear the wreckage, you will find love
Love and hope from our God above

If you will look you will find it there
Don't leave it buried it's meant to share

Love's more than pleasure, Love's pure joy
Love's the hand of Hope, this world can't destroy

There's a hidden treasure inside your heart
Prayer and meditation is the place to start

Greg Wooley

Letting Go

Letting God; I'm letting go
Holding on, we just can't grow

He whispers fly, yet I fear
My eyes grow misty, with a tear

I'm a failure, I'm sure You know
"It's in the past, now let it go"

Take the present as a gift
Just let go and make the shift

Shift your focus, shift your eyes
Make reality your paradise

Our new manager is who God is
When I let go and I am His

The pressure's off, the stress is gone
Accept the gift of the new day's dawn

Choose to let God and then begin to grow
I pray today is the day that you will let go

Victor

Lord make me your instrument and then put me in
tune
Help me overcome every defect of character that
has brought me to ruin

Produce in me the harmony You would have me to
bring
From victim to victor is Your song that I sing

In my own ways and my thinking my life turns
insane
Make me Your instrument so that none of old can
remain

Thorn

A thorn in our side, a rock in our shoe
We all have our obstacles that's nothing new

Stumbling blocks become stepping stones to help us
move higher
To learn from our mistakes should be our goal and
our greatest desire

Let me look at failure and rejection with an eye to
help me to see
It's through trial, error and adjust, I am making the
most out of me

A rock in my shoe, a thorn in my side
Real learning happens when success and failure
collide

The Fight

Out of the darkness and into the light
We can't get through the dirt without fighting the
fight

So many things we can't sit back and just take for
granted
Hope's seeds won't grow themselves once they've
been planted

It takes sunshine and spirit to push through the dirt
We won't really get rooted until we let go of the
hurt

Out of the darkness and into the light
An oak will remain an acorn if it don't fight the
fight

Greg Wooley

Spirit of Inspiration

I am a candle lighter and I start the burn
I share inspiration as I live and I learn

I am the light and I start the fire
I fan the flames into burning desire

I unleash the purpose and I unlock the why
I bring out the greatness in everything that I try

This world isn't dying from a lack of information
What we are lacking is the Spirit of Inspiration

What use is the direction without the will to climb
I'll light the candles my friend and It's Firing Time

Doubt My Doubt

Do you know you have value, your life has its worth
God had you in mind before the time of your birth

This world is unfair and all too often its cruel
It takes some abrasiveness to polish a jewel

The bible promises for us that love God all things will work for our good
So many times it is better to understand that than to be understood

You have great worth whether you're with or without
Today I will believe my beliefs and I will doubt my doubt

Whole

Filling the hole by becoming part of the whole
It seemed I was born missing part of my soul

Becoming a part of something greater than me
Mysteriously filled the void and I was set free

It wasn't until I began to try to practice God's
principles in all my affairs
Was I able to see past me, my worries and let God
manage my cares

But by setting new boundaries they had the opposite
effect and that seemed odd
I could have a new freedom and new hope when I
tried to be more like my God

Free at Last

The gift of serenity and the gift of peace of mind
Are the gifts of the spirit when it's God will I find

Searching for answers and searching for love
Every why leads me back to my God above

I once was so lost and now I have been found
As I step closer to God, my chains come unbound

Though once I sought money and once I sought
power
When God let me find everything in nothing was
my finest hour

The greatest of gifts was being set free
I had God's Grace and Love just because I was me

I gave Him the future and let go of the past
I'm not possessed by my obsessions, I am free at
last

Willingness

Hurting is the fuel, willingness the key
Acceptance is the door to setting ourselves free

God I ask for a new awareness to where I've been so
blind
I know my life won't truly change until you've
changed my mind

In and under my own power I get in the rinse and
repeat
I surrender in my insanity it's brought me to defeat

Hurting is the fuel and willingness the key
I long for transformation to make the most out of
me

Remove Your Shade

You are a light so remove your shade
God thought of you when you were made

Troubles came and troubles went
At times our trouble is heaven sent

Eyes off this world and on the Source
It's by our light God plots our course

You are a light so remove your shade
We will grow when the foundation's laid

Stepping stones are made from stumbling blocks
I pray today that you will drop those those rocks

Eyes off this world and back on Him
Look to God when we're growing dim

You are a light so remove your shade
Plug back in when the light seems to fade

Whether we're growing old or we are brand new
There's a light that's meant to shine in me and you

It's our own thinking that becomes our cloud
We make our shadow when we are to proud

You are a light so remove your shade
Walk with God our Light will never fade

G.O.D

It was in and through Good Orderly Direction I
made my new start
To dare to believe I might mend the pieces of this
broken heart

With the concept of a power greater than myself I
started to wrestle
That anything of value might come from the pieces
of this broken vessel

These broken pieces of what had become me
Would they be of any use to a G.O.D

A god for which I had no faith and seemed had no
use for me
The door to faith eased open in the form of a
G.O.D.

In the darkest of days there is a place the lost are
found and the trash become treasure
Where harmonious action replaces our gut reaction
and serenity becomes the way that we measure

We learn to laugh at ourselves and break the chains
of our thinking
You see the root of our problem wasn't the drugs
and wasn't the drinking   *(continued >)*

The root problem is a malady of the spirit and from
God we were so far adrift
Then a Group of Drunks offered the grace they'd
been given as His free gift

A gift I didn't deserve and that I could never repay
A gift that if I were to keep it I had to give it away

Sobriety and salvation are true gifts that we keep by
giving
If I would do what you do, I could have what you
have; a new way of living

Some find Him in a flash, others in time of
reflection
As for me I found the path in Good Orderly
Direction

Author Biography

Greg Wooley has been in the self-help field for over twenty-five years. That's when the journey to overcome a seemingly hopeless and helpless state of mind started.

He has found victory over addiction and depression. One of the best ways to stay on the hope filled path is by helping others to find their way to hope as well. Helping others find hope is where Greg has found his purpose and passion.

He truly hopes these poetic gems will help take your eyes off the problems and shine some light on the solutions. He has written personal poems for keepsakes, vows and presents.

He has also partnered with pastors to use his poems in their sermons and growth messages. Greg would love to hear from you and is very interested in finding ways to share in shining the light of hope together. His life is a great testimony of hope, healing and overcoming the odds.

Greg love's building and growing communities for both personal and professional growth. Like-minded people with like-minded goals is where real life change happens! Visit and contact him at www.GregWooley.com.

Ordering Information

Greater Ways Publishing
PO Box 701017
St. Cloud, FL 34770
roofinflorida@aol.com
www.GregWooley.com

Gems from G.O.D.
ISBN: 978-1-7339478-9-3
(paperback)

Made in the USA
Columbia, SC
17 June 2019